LAURA HILLS-GARNER

'UPSTAIRS'

Preface

I developed cPTSD (Complex Post Traumatic Stress Disorder) and GAD, (Generalised Anxiety Disorder) at the age of 27 years old and to be blunt it left me reeling. It has been a long, hard journey (I hate the word journey!) of therapy and self-discovery to get to a healthier place. Writing has been a constant companion through the years and a form of therapy in itself. I wanted to share my story in the hope that it may help others make sense of theirs. I've certainly not made recovery look elegant and have a long road ahead, but I catch glimpses of myself and continue to see a better version looking back. If I've learnt anything along the way:

1) Recovery IS possible
2) Ask for help

3) You have to let yourself feel to heal

4) Fear exists in the future and regret in the past- there is much solace in the present

5) There is no magic wand

6) Recovery is not linear- you're allowed to trip over

7) Keep moving forward no matter how small the steps

8) No-one else can fix you

9) You have to be stubborn and determined

10) You are <u>worth it</u>

Sharing my story is a big step. Thankyou sincerely for taking the time to read it and I hope it touches you in some way.

To all those struggling... keep fighting, you're not alone.

L-H-G

'Upstairs' was inspired by a poem with the same title, written by me over 15 years ago. The poem lay dormant in a folder as it never felt 'finished'. I now know this was because there was more for me to say...

Upstairs 2001

Upstairs in this big old house, I patiently walk the floors
Tediously I pace the floorboards, grappling with locked doors
I hear them knocking inquisitively, trying to get in
Peeping through the letter box, to glimpse the realms within
A big effort to venture 'upstairs' passing room to room
Each one filled with memories of pain and former doom
Spoken words flash before me, bouncing from wall to ceiling
I stand within the doorway, numb yet full of feeling
A jumbled maze lies before me and noise fills my ears
The ticking clock grows louder only noticed in recent years
Safe within my annexe, doors bolted from within

*"Safe as houses", they say. but keeping them out or
me in?*

*Nagging wind rattles the windows and the world
outside goes by*

*On my repetitive circuit, well-worn floorboards
groan and sigh*

*The layers of peeling wallpaper are no guise for
rising damp*

*The dank and dinghy atmosphere is not bettered by a
lamp*

In no fit state for visitors, upstairs is an awful mess

*My dirty laundry upon the line and maintenance to
address*

Sparse walls once decorated with cherished portraits

*Which now sit faded in boxes as if they knew their
fates*

*An unintelligible dialogue, the echoes don't make
sense or rhyme*

*When I find a safe route to pass, the layout changes
every time*

Konstantina,

Thankyou will never be enough.

Laura Hills-Garner

This is a book to be read with the mind, not just the eyes. Savour each hand-picked word and carved sentence. The ink and pages are the only thing that is Black and White.

;

I grip the handrail tightly, my hand blending in with the pale, glossy wood. I squidge my toes into the soft, spongy fabric beneath my feet, taking comfort in the solid edges of the stairs beneath me. I glance behind at the neat and ordered living room, bookcase bulging with well-thumbed books and open fireplace, rustic and inviting. I take a huge lungful of the rooms scent; Candle fragrance, incense and toast, smells which to others might mean burnt wax, artificial air-freshener and mouldy bread, but to me, mean home.

I look up at the unobtrusive White door before me and the stairs between us marking the mammoth climb ahead. The stairs appear to grow in depth before my eyes, and I'm certain there are more today than there were yesterday. I reluctantly pad up the stairs, pausing at the top allowing the effects of the minor exertion to pass. The cool, shiny, orb-like door handle offers an almost regal assurance, its unexpected warmth striking against my ghostly hand. My temple throbs with what can only be a mini, bouncing trampolinist doing damage inside my skull.

I take a deep breath and twist the handle. It turns easily in my hand but as I nudge the door there is an unexpected, foreboding resistance. I let out a sigh and glance behind me. I could easily run away, to the safe and familiar below, but no......I mustn't.... I've been doing that for too long.

When I was little, 'Upstairs' was a mystical treasure-trove just waiting to be explored. A limitless land of imagination and make-believe, where every story had a happy ending, good triumphed over evil and as long as you did your best and minded your manners, everything would be okay. Where Santa still existed, your parents could fix anything and a bearded, sandalled man was in the sky watching over us. Over time, the corners of 'Upstairs' grew darker, the corridors longer and more unfamiliar and I began to wander the expanse with trepidation rather than curiosity. As my bones grew, my fear of 'upstairs' grew also and it became my 'monster under the bed', like the dark corner of the garden you look twice at before running past, no matter your age. Shadows would dance upon the walls, eager to consume me and I felt dwarfed by its expanse, convinced I would never find my way out. The unknown was no longer exciting, but frightening. As the years went by, I found excuses to avoid going 'Upstairs' and if I ever had to venture there, would hurry through, fixated on the toes upon my feet. Now, here I stand, poised before the wooden door, the only thing standing between me and an unknown world which frightens yet intrigues me.

I turn the handle once more and push the door with both hands, my gnarled knuckles glinting in the light as the door groans with objection. I glance back at the distant bottom step, too far to go back now. I lunge against the door with the full weight of my body and it swings open with horror movie creak.

I stand within the doorway, my stomach a bubbling cauldron of acid, popping candy fizzing at my throat. My body a human barometer; heat rises from my toes to my forehead, leaving behind a clammy, pallid film. Warm, thin saliva floods my mouth and I glance around habitually for a receptacle, clamping my hand tightly over my mouth, yet relax slightly as I remember there is no-one here to see me come undone.

Images of the staircase behind me giving way, marooning me with nothing but the echoes flash before my eyes and I have to check to see it's still there. My feet remain anchored to the floor by an invisible magnetic force. I pull down the sleeves of my ill-fitting shirt to cover my exposed arms and the tiny bumps appearing on my arms. My senses begin to awaken and I crinkle my eyes together, willing them to make sense of the gloomy darkness before me. There is a stale, musty, sour smell and I breathe through my mouth to stem the odorous intrusion. The air is thick and warm, and I swallow it begrudgingly in gulps, taking in my surroundings.

As my eyes adjust, I see I am in a dank, dimly lit room flowing into a sea of infinite blackness. Distressed, ill-fitting floor boards snake a rough path across the room, gaps disappear into the abyss below. An old dresser loiters in the corner, drawers dribbling their remains and doors hanging open as if their contents left in a hurry.... People have been here. They clearly didn't stick around and left things in a mess.

Spewing, stacked boxes disguise a haphazard walkway leading to the far wall which is partially concealed by a curious yellowed and crusty canvas sheeting; an ominous veil concealing the wall behind. The canvas intrigues me, but something tells me I don't want to know what's behind there. There is no discernible noise, except the beating within my chest and yet it is deafening.

I lift my concrete foot and take a tentative step forward, the wood groaning beneath my foot. To the side of me, a flicker of movement catches my eye and I freeze. A book sits atop a bulging box, its pages flapped open, as if turned by an invisible hand. I stoop to make out the words written upon the page and they glare back at me with a poignant finality…. 'The End'.

I shiver and a fizzy rash prickles the base of my neck. Using legs that are no longer my own, I stumble forward, I can almost feel my bottom teeth receding with the pressure of those above, but with grim determination I turn, pulling the door closed behind me and wrestle the seven stubborn locks, preventing both entry and exit. I place my hand and forehead upon the wooden door mustering warmth from the other side and notice that I am barefoot. Ill prepared I turn to face my nemesis with a sad resignation, an electric current alternates erratically inside me with each step, rendering me a clumsy and awkward string-less puppet without kneecaps. I clench my hands in a vain hope of dispelling the fizzing in my fingers. My tongue a dry slab of granite, my tonsils swollen, rough husks as I try swallowing the wave that threatens to choke me.

Gingerly, I extend searching hands into the air before me and recoil as my fingers glance against something smooth. Faded smiley faces hug the wall, a stark contrast in this desperate environment. I run my hands over the smooth paper and a loose corner flaps against my fingers which twitch reflexively. I tug at the

loose corner, the paper peels cleanly like skin
after sunburn and I smile with satisfaction as it
comes free in one piece, dwarfing me beneath it,
revealing another layer of cheery, childish
wallpaper. Erratically I pull strip after strip
from the wall and deftly sidestep the chunk of
plaster that follows the last layer, covering me
with gritty snow, giving my dull, boring brown
hair grey highlights.

The discarded layers clamber at my ankles as I
inspect what I have unveiled. Cracks spider the
undressed, exposed wall and a jagged, gaping,
hole snarls at me from the centre. I cautiously
poke at the hole with my index finger, tearing it
away quickly from the clutches of the draughty
unknown. I snatch at the discarded paper at
my feet and stuff it untidily back into the hole.
I stand back to survey my handiwork with

hands on hips and laugh to myself at my ingenuity; no-one will even notice!

I edge across the room, stroking the wall for reassurance against the uneven floor. Branches tap at the windows; the nagging wind reminding me of the world outside oblivious to my peril.

The whisperings of muttering, insistent voices echo across the dismal landscape, lacerating my brain. The room before me shrinks with each step, leading into a long dark passage. Doors stand proudly to attention on either side. I shuffle along, turning each handle half-heartedly as I go, undecided as to whether I want them to open. Some are unlocked but have swollen over the years and resist me, and some are locked and perhaps always will be. The final door bursts open with persuasion and showers me with a deluge of disregarded souvenirs. I nudge at the contents of the huge pile with my foot; among it a naked dolly, empty pill bottles, Elvis records and more beer bottles than I could count. I usher the contents out of sight back into the cupboard and jostle with the door pushing back at me. I continue on, avoiding the desperate darkness in the corners as the hallway opens out to a small square room. Four chairs sit around an upended dining table whilst dinner plate remnants and broken glass confetti the floor. White squares dot the walls at intervals where pictures once hung with pride, now glaringly absent. The passageway opens out onto a long tunnel-like corridor, corners rounded by shadows. I look left, then right kneading the taught, elastic band stretched across my shoulders. Neither way looks welcoming, but I turn left and immediately pause mid-step, frozen like a musical statue. I hear something…

With frantic effort, my brain endeavours to translate the noise into something meaningful. I edge along the corridor, intrigued yet afraid I won't be able to 'unhear' the noise. Strains of a faint melody echo down the hall. It is disturbing yet I am drawn to it like a car-crash, pulling me closer into a vortex. The haunting, familiar tune is unbelievably moving, and I feel its grip reaching down my throat and squeezing my heart. With each furtive step its grip increases and I am compelled towards it. Somehow, I know if I immerse myself in this sombre tune it will consume me forever, yet my kamikaze feet sabotage my ability to stop. As I meander through the wreckage before me, a sharp pain explodes in my right foot severing the melodic connection. I stumble against the wall, clutching one foot in the air in a gymnast pose I would struggle to repeat. I squeeze everything shut and hold my breath feigning ignorance. I peek through one eye and spy a large shard of glass protruding proudly from my big toe. I yank at the foreign object, gritting my teeth against pain that doesn't come and slide my thumb over warm stickiness. I was wrong to come. 'I should be downstairs doing something useful' I think to myself. I call up the 'to-do' list I carry in my mind for such occasions and imagine my self-worth inflating with each thing I tick off the list and resign myself to leaving immediately before I really do any damage. My shirt sticks to my underarms like clingfilm. "Just keep moving" I mutter to myself and unsticking my thumb from my toe I hobble forward drunkenly on the nine good toes I have left. I walk blindly, ignoring the seaweed-like entities clutching at my feet and the urge to run.

I can no longer tell where I am or where I have been as I stagger from room to room. Loose plaster rains down upon me as I bump aimlessly through the hallways. The walls lean over me menacingly as I collapse into the corner; my sticky skin tinged with filth and the smell of my fear emanating from my pores disgusts me. I am soiled, dirty, defeated and lost.... but I *will not cry*. I take a deep breath, rise up and as I turn the corner a vocal cacophony breaks my consciousness.... A voice......beckons to me, calling my name. I propel myself off the wall stumbling and weaving across the room into the next and stop short. My eyes scan a blatantly empty room and I frown in confusion. Again, the voice calls to me. It is close. Wait!" I shout; mobilising my aching limbs, I cross the room, spiralling through the doorway into the next. I chase through room after room following the calling voice, but no matter how quickly my limbs scissor beneath me I never seem to make any ground. I stop out of breath and exhausted, a sheen of sweat glosses my forehead. I slide down the crumbling wall to the floor, head in hands as I endeavour to regain control of my breath. I look around the room and my eyes fall upon the draped, Yellowed canvas sheeting, the grimy curtain hanging at the window and the scrunched wallpaper protruding from the hole in the wall. I let out a joyful yelp that I wouldn't want anyone to hear as my eyes alight on the outline of the door that will lead me out of this labyrinth. I jump up instantly and run for the door before anyone can move it and rip at the locks one by one, tearing my fingernails in the process. I snap the handle down and wrench the door wide, raising my arm in protection against the brightness. I slam the door closed behind me and chase black spots around my field of vision that reminds me of the 80's computer game, Pong. I rest my back on the door, closing my eyes as my pulse returns to its regular, erratic rhythm. My swollen heart threatens to burst the puny cage encasing it. I grip the handrail and descend to safety not noticing the crimson, smudged kisses I leave on the top step as I leave. Next time…. I will come prepared I admonish myself.

The following week I find myself contemplating the stairs once again. This time a warm glow radiates heat from my stomach, rendering the bannister edges softer and a welcome bravado spurs me on. I weave up the spongy stairs and smash the door defiantly as I barge it open. Dust falls from the ceiling in protestation as I swagger into the room, fists clenched glowering at the dust particles from bloodshot eyes. I stomp down the hallway, leaning into the opposing force of the tilting floor. My inner compass fails me, but my faithful feet lead me on, turning this time right at the fork in the corridor. I navigate hordes of rubbish that I should have let go long ago; reams and reams of paper, photos and things I don't even recognise anymore. I pass closed doors but apprehensive to go too far from the beaten track I continue on, eventually emerging onto a landing facing a single White door.

The door is different to any others I have passed so far. Though also wooden, it appears to be a front door with frosted glass panel and the number '26' tacked to the wood. The number 6 hangs precariously at an angle. The letter box creaks as I pinch it open slowly. I bend down to peer through and an acrid, sickly smell of rot and decay assaults my nostrils through the yellowed net curtain. My stomach knots and gags uncontrollably in protest and moisture shocks my burning cheeks. My eyes widen in alarm as my insides threaten to escape before I can. My mind is already running down the corridor I came from, adrenalin floods my arms and legs, but quicksand eats me from the soles upwards, my stupid legs hanging prone below me. Warmth trickles down the inside of my leg and darkness reaches across the denim of my jeans. My insides and outside jangle out of synch with each other until finding some semblance of unison and reigniting the relationship with my limbs, I lurch back down the hallway, hand clamped over my mouth, grimacing at the bitter taste on my fingers. I stumble through overflowing rooms, endeavouring to avoid the malicious clutches of the rubbish at my feet. I pause, breathless, at the end of a narrow, dimly lit corridor. Doors line either side of the corridor, reaching out into the darkness beyond. I begin to edge my way along the narrow space, shuffling sideways past the obstacles littering the constricted walkway. As I pass the first door, I feel something grasp at my body. I look down to see unfamiliar hands clamouring at me through the darkness. I grimace at the insistent clutches of the probing fingers that grapple at my clothes and belt buckle. Gravity pulls at my soles, weighing me down as they ransack each crevice of my clothes, pockets and body. I turn my face away from the warm, sickly breath that brushes my cheek, tinged with stale smoke and beer and watch shamefully from the ceiling at the immobilised body below, crawling with unwanted guests. I can no longer feel the hands clutching at me from my place of safety, in fact I can no longer feel anything. I just watch, emotionless and empty, wondering if this is how it feels to be dead. One by one, the hands finally withdraw and I float back down to assume my seat at the controls, free to move uninhibited once more. I brush at my clothes, soiled with grubby handprints that only I can see. At the end of the hallway, in thick black paint, erratically scrawled writing reads:

PISSED

TWAT

SUCKS

DICK

I fruitlessly scrub at the vulgar lettering and
search frantically for something to cover it up,
but there is nothing. I look down at my now
black, stained hands with shame and leave the
corridor, desperate to put as much distance
between myself and the murky mural.

Bulging filing cabinets join formation, spitting
files at me as I enter the next room and I can
make out something suspended in the back
corner. I gingerly step towards what looks
faintly like carcasses swinging in an abattoir
and gape in horror. Swinging against the
crumbling backdrop are 3 bodies, hanging from

their necks, upturned chairs laying beneath them. I run frenzied towards the first body, taking the limp legs in my arms in desperation and lifting with all my might, trying desperately to relieve the pressure that is cutting off the air. I look at the other two bodies and attempt to gather all three within my arms, but they are too heavy for me to lift alone. I sink down to my knees, feeling helpless and a failure, knowing…. I cannot save them. Though I have torn my face away from them, the image of the 3 has scorched my mind and no matter how many times I blink, I cannot lose that image. I feel it pulling at the frayed edges of my mind.

I run out of the room trying to put distance between me and the futility of the image, swallowing the lump in my throat that tells me…. I cannot save them. As I turn the corner, I stop still in my tracks…… There, before me standing defiantly once again…. number 26.

I shake my head from side to side and tear at my hair in desperation. The engine in the pit of my stomach revs, ready to transport me and I run aimlessly through room after room, yet each path I take seems to lead me right back to that door…….number 26. I lash out at the walls grating my knuckles against the abrasive brickwork and slump down to the floor like a heap of discarded clothes. A storm is raging.

Out of the corner of my eye I see something glinting amongst the rubble. I snatch at it, screwing one eye closed to make sense of the blurry, jagged piece of metal in my hand. My saccharine breath steams the mirror, blurring the reflection looking back at me and my stomach turns as stale alcohol bounces back to my nostrils from my breath. I look at the unrecognisable face before me, - the puffy eyes, large pupils and gaunt, pale face. I close my eyes, but the image imprints the inside of my eyelids. I grip the mirror, squeezing with all my might to crush it into dust and watch the warm scarlet blood snake between my fingers, pooling into my palm. I look on with envy, in awe of the crude simplicity, expressing more in that drip than I ever could.

I lean my head against the cigarette scented wall, noticing a slow, rhythmic vibration through the bricks and roll to my knees. calves cramping in protest. A clock hangs from the wall above, slicing at the air with each tick, getting louder with each second that passes. The pendulum waves at me gloating with each swing, a haunting reminder of time draining away, of the minutes going by without me in attendance. I throw the bloodied mirror into its smirking face; watching as the clock dangles stubbornly and drops to the floor, rendered silent at last. I turn victoriously to move away but freeze disbelievingly mid-step.... Tick... tick... tick.... it taunts me, determined to have the last word. I lift my leg, ready to silence its relentless goading forever. Ready to smash it to smithereens when......a persistent tapping cuts through the long echoey corridors to find my ears. Tilting my head to one side, frowning in disbelief........ 'it can't be' I mutter to myself. Again, seven taps resound through the halls and I follow their echo, a prominent crease carving up my forehead. My pulse quickens, and wiping the bloody, blackened hands down the front of my jeans I follow the noise down twists and turns; my mind jostling with the threat of expectancy. I make my way back to the entryway and peel back the grimy curtain and wipe the filthy pane with the sleeve of my shirt. The window-pane plants a shocking kiss upon my forehead as I strain to identify the originator of the noise.

I do not recognise the small figure on the front step below. She stands bright and vibrant, shiny shoes planted firmly and reaches on tip-toes to knock again. I cower into the safety of the curtain as the noise reverberates around the house towards me, I feel whatever holds my eyes in place stretching as they consume the little figure below. I watch with interest, apprehension, conflicted.

My shoulders drop in relief and I let out my first breath in minutes as she turns and strides confidently down the overgrown pathway away from the house. I watch intently as she reaches the end, pauses and turns. Her eyes dart to the window where I stand and I shrink back letting the fabric drop into place, feeling the intensity of her gaze through the bricks and wallpaper. It is as if she knew I was there all along.

The following week, I steel myself to venture upstairs once again, determined to start to make some order of the chaos. I resolve to staying in the first room, keeping the door firmly in my sights. Stacks of boxes loom over me, wobbling precariously and I amble like a lost child, moving boxes from one place to another seemingly doing more harm than good. Opening one box, leads to another and to another and I don't even know where to start.

Overwhelmed by the multiplying boxes before me I sit against the wall defeated, berating myself for my inadequacy when I am jolted back to reality by a knock at the front door. I cross to the window and peer through the curtain to see the same girl standing on the step below. She stands in stark, colourful contrast to the unattractive house, ignoring the unwelcoming, unkempt pathway and dirty laundry on the line with a brazen disregard. She waits patiently and then turns and wanders down the pathway once again. This time, I do not hide myself behind the curtain, yet she doesn't look back and I am strangely.... disappointed.

My journeys upstairs become a weekly ritual. I climb the stairs each Wednesday never making it much further than the entryway. At 10:30

each week there is a knock at the front door that goes unanswered. Regardless, the girl returns stubbornly each week and I spend the days between wondering why. She becomes a welcome interruption that I watch through diluted eyes each week, with curiosity and a little terror.

One afternoon as I prepare to watch her leave once more I am drawn to something on the old side-table by the window next to me. I pick up the dusty book and wipe the leather-bound cover with my sleeve. Etched in faded, gold writing are the words 'Hopes and Dreams'. I open the book and choke on the breath in my throat. There on the first page is a picture of a smiling girl with an alluring carefree cheekiness. The book slaps the floor, exploding dust as it falls from my hand and the girl turns to begin her retreat down the path and I know what I have to do. I swing open the door, leaping down the stairs, moving too rapidly to allow thinking or feeling and grab the door handle, wrenching it open. She must have gone by now, surely......

As the door swings open framing the petite figure at the end of the path, time slows. A thudding percussion beats through every inch of my body as if I have swallowed a thousand hearts, all beating to escape. I shut my mouth, ears, nostrils and clench every muscle to keep from spilling out onto the pathway. Slowly, she turns to face me and the corners of her mouth lift imperceptibly. My eyes busy themselves counting grass stems and I shuffle from one foot to the other determining why I felt this was a good idea. My mind is blank, my body hangs like a dress on a hanger below me. She strides down the path and stops a few paces before me, watching me intently. My eyes dart from her to the sky, to her, to the floor, to her, to the grass, to her, to the gate, to her and I assimilate an image of her in my mind with the snapshots I grab.

She is pretty with olive skin and dark brown hair in ringlets and intense, dark, brown eyes that burn. She is small yet the enormity of her scares me and I grip hold of the door to disguise my trembling hands. The wind bites at my neck, crawling up my spine and I have to glance downwards to check that I am clothed. My cheeks flush as I notice my bare, battered feet and I feel see-through as she looks at me with something quite unrecognisable and though she stands there in silence, it feels as though she is screaming at me. I am not sure what I'm supposed to do, I feel sick and a familiar ache across my forehead informs me that I am frowning and crushing my teeth into my jaw. Surely.... She doesn't want to come in? I think to myself. I shuffle awkwardly on my feet and push the door ajar raising my eyebrows at her in question, fearing her response. She nods nonchalantly and strides past me with confidence as the arid cracks branching across my tongue plead for me to close my mouth.

She glides around the living room, bending to look at pictures, books, ornaments and medals that adorn the room, touching nothing, her face giving nothing away. She turns periodically and smiles at me, her eyes prodding at me like fingers, and I smile at the piece of wall 2cm above her head. I am desperate to look into her eyes but that would mean letting her look into mine. After completing a circuit of the room, she makes her way back towards me and stops at the bottom of the stairs. I take a step back from her, needing a small reprieve from the intensity that seems to burn between us, hoping she cannot hear my raging heart. She lifts her arm and points upwards to the door above, tilting her head to one side. I shake my head violently and she smiles gently but points again to the top of the stairs. I shake my head again and she nods, takes a small step back and sits down on the circular rug in the centre of the living room. She points to a photo album sitting on the cabinet and I reluctantly hand it to her taking care not to brush her small hands, perfectly painted with coral nail varnish. I feel like a giant awkward ogre as we sit side by side flicking through the thick pages, sharing the treasure of my childhood. Warmth radiates through me as I devour the pictures; Mum carrying me across a sea of fallen leaves as we wear matching, bobbly jumpers, Dad holding me in the air in his big, strong hands, me displaying proudly the Red skateboard he spent hours making, my sister and I stood back-to-back as we model matching neon outfits, handstitched by Mum. I revel in the snapshots of Christmases, Halloween and birthdays marked by homemade cakes, creative costumes, laughter and happiness until we reach the end and I reluctantly close the album. She nods at me, stands and indicates the purple watch decorating her dainty wrist. It is ten-to-twelve. She turns and strides to the front door. "Wait!" I say, placing the album on the floor, getting to my feet and rushing to the door... but she has already gone, as quickly as she arrived. "I don't even know who you are" … I whisper into the wind.

I close the door and expel the depths of my lungs to the room which suddenly feels very empty without her. I run to the sink expelling pitiful dribble from my empty spasming stomach and rinse my mouth. I shuffle, foot to foot, not quite knowing what to do with myself. 'Did that really happen'? I think to myself. Returning to the living room I notice the photo album upon the flow, the only evidence of her presence. I return it to its shelf and lie on the sofa, squeezing my eyes against the pressure building behind them. I screw my face into the soft contours of the cushion, trying to cram the moisture leaking from my eyes back in, a strange, guttural noise comes from the cushion.

I have rattled around here for years alone and been 'fine', and yet only now, after letting someone in do I feel the loneliest I've ever felt.

The following week I busy myself pretending not to watch the heavy hands of the clock tick closer to 10:30. The urge to leave and the bubbling acidic stomach contents rise with each revolution of the hand. I berate myself with each glance towards the door and pace the kitchen, feeling like a school girl, embarrassed of the horrible, unfamiliar sensation I have in my stomach. Voices bounce violently off the walls of my skull; "Why would she come back to see you!" they shout at me. I enter a futile exchange with a formidable opponent, knowing it is a fruitless argument. I reflect on her previous visit and can't shake the notion that in that small exchange, I didn't offer her or give her anything...... Why would she come back?

An insistent tapping drowns out my pitiful response. I run to the door and pause to prevent my rasping breath from betraying me. She is wearing the same brightly coloured dress, curly hair cascading over her shoulders and waits patiently as my eyes gradually find their way to hers. She smiles, and I offer a crooked smile back, my teeth feeling oversized in my mouth and I look away. I open the door and I follow her inside exploring the fabric crevices of my pockets for something that might help me with the situation. Drawing a blank I walk to the kitchen, remove a glass from the cupboard and fill it with water. I gulp it down, twisting my head to hide the escaped liquid that runs down my face. My mouth aches in thanks and the cool water branches out, soothing my body. I look at her, pointing to the tap but she shakes her head and smiles. I pull the cupboard ajar shielding her eyes from the sparse contents inside and snatch at a packet of biscuits, thrusting them at her like a weapon. She shakes her head and smiles again. I look round the house x-raying the cupboards knowing full well I have nothing more to offer her. She turns and walks to the bottom of the stairs, looks up at the door and back at me. I shake my head at her and drop my eyes to the floor feeling her eyes boring into me. 'She's too nice for upstairs' I think to myself and lift my eyes, half hoping she will have disappeared, knowing I wouldn't be surprised if she had, but she's still there. I take a step closer and place my hand on the bannister. She prods me on with a little nod of her head as my legs move mechanically below me, eyes trained on the door above.

I reach half way up the stairs and my legs cease to co-operate. I wrestle in frustration against the invisible wall hampering my progress, preventing me from moving forward. I flinch at the soft touch on my shoulder blade and my mind warps with the realisation that whatever is touching me is connected to her arm! Her hand, resting gently but firmly on the top of my shoulder burning through my shirt propels me forward towards the door, not pushing, but a solid, constant pressure. When we reach the top, she nods, holds up her finger and turns to head back down the stairs. My hand reaches out inadvertently towards her, freezing in mid-air. She turns, nods and smiles and continues walking down the stairs. She throws open the wicker basket by the front door, reaches in and returns to me clutching a pair of soft, fluffy slippers. She gestures for me to sit on the top step and I look at her questioningly. She points to the carpet in front of the door, peppered with red marks trodden into the carpet. I frown at her, shrugging my shoulders, giving my best 'I didn't do it' face, she smiles, pointing down at my feet. In confusion I bend to inspect my foot and am shocked to see my battered soles, lined with cuts and scrapes. I notice matching purple marks and scratches on my knees and elbows which I can only link to my recent visits 'upstairs'. A volume switch is flicked as my eyes sweep across each battered part of my body. Every inch seems to suddenly ache with a pain I hadn't realised I had, as if I had undergone a full body X-ray and the knocks and bruises are suddenly painfully apparent. I lift my damaged feet and place them in the soft, warm slippers and stand up to face her. She nods at the door and I open it slowly, dressed for battle.

As the door opens, I fight the urge to cover her eyes, squeezing my arms firmly against my sides for fear of pushing her down the stairs, away from the darkness that greets us. The dinginess and destruction is more prevalent in her shadow, yet her face betrays nothing as I search for evidence of disgust or horror. I follow behind through the hallways as she wanders round inquisitively, following a map she doesn't share with me. I watch her every move a little in awe of the bravery and fierceness she exudes and her beauty is intensified by the dismal scenery.

I watch her from afar as she stops and crosses the room, picks up an abandoned box in the corner and upends the contents onto the floor with abandon. She repeats this until 3 empty boxes sit before us. I grimace at the dirty smudges that soil her beautiful dress as she kneels in front of the boxes. She takes out a pen and on the front of each box she writes:

'no longer needed', 'not yours' and 'to be sorted'

I look at her questioningly and she gestures for me to sort my stuff into the appropriate boxes. She waits patiently as I lift each item, looking at her for reassurance as I realise, I have no idea where anything should go. Some items I hold for an age, reluctant to let go and some I cast aside unsure where they truly belong but mostly, I look for the box labelled 'mine'.

When the boxes are full she stands up shaking the dust off her skirt and picks up the 'not yours' box. I follow her back through the hallways to the entryway. She pauses, placing the box on the floor and walks over to the far wall. She eyes the dried-out old canvas sheet draped across the breadth of the wall that I had noticed in my first visit. She reaches her hand out towards the edge of the sheet and I scurry over, placing myself between her and the canvas. I look directly in her eye shaking my head and she stumbles backwards. I marvel incredulously at the force of my super-power eye contact until I look down and see my arms outstretched towards her and realise....I pushed her. I look into her eyes and for the first time do not break eye contact as a silent tear flows down my cheek. She nods and lifting her arm shows me the purple watch.... it's 11:50. She picks up the box and skips down the stairs. I hear the front door click and only then stop staring at my hands. I make my way to the window, pull back the curtain and watch as she strides down the path, no evidence of struggle despite the large load she's carrying.

The following week at 10:25, I wear out the carpet of the living room knowing that there will be no visitors today and knowing that it is my own fault. I watch the hands tick closer to proving me right. I chastise myself for pushing her but chastise myself more for letting her in to begin with. She should never have come here! Stupid girl!. My skin jumps an inch away from my bones as a tapping breaks the silence of the room. I edge the door open, peering around it in disbelief and…. There she is. She strides in past me and I follow her up the stairs putting on my slippers as I go. She leads me down corridors until I hear the familiar strains of the sad soundtrack. I want to clamp my hands over her ears to prevent the music infiltrating her bones and tainting her in some way, but she ploughs on seemingly unaffected. We follow the music into a room where a radio sits on the table by the wall. She pauses, listening intently, her face nondescript then looks up at me, eyebrows raised. I nod. She reaches down and turns the station and melodious, uplifting music spills from the radio across the room, cutting through the dense air of the room. Poignant words burst from the speakers; a soundtrack to my soul echoed back at me. The words infiltrate my mind and heart and I blush with the affinity I have with them. Each word strips me bare, recounting everything I wish I could say or hear. She smiles and begins to sway side to side stirring the air with her fingers, her head thrown back in carefree abandon. She opens her eyes and points at the floor in front of her. I shrink back in horror, shaking my head, frowning, crossing my arms in front of me. She smiles, pointing down at my body. I look down and notice that I am swaying involuntarily in time to the music; a tree bending with the breeze. My mouth spasms and I cannot control the muscles in my face as they fight to house the invisible coat hanger lodged there. I unravel the alien arms clamped in front of me, hold them out and helicopter round gazing at the ceiling. I look to the girl for reassurance, but she is mirroring my spinning action and smiling. I stop noticing my gangly legs, two giant left feet and lanky body that lies like a slab of meat below me as I spin round the room. A light, raucous noise startles me and I realise.... it is coming from me.

We leave the music playing and spill out into the hall, cheeks flushed and slightly out of breath. I follow her through the halls until we are back at the entrance way. She looks across at the far wall with the canvas sheeting in place and looks back at me head tilted to the side. I walk over to the wall and nod at her reluctantly. She reaches out and takes a corner of the canvas and glances at me. I nod again. Gently she tugs and the canvas breaks free dropping a curtain of dust across the room. I blink frantically through the haze and as the dust settles I can make out an empty picture frame hanging on the wall. She looks at me, nods and smiles and I look back at her frowning. She reaches into her pocket and brings out a bright, white tissue. She leans up on tiptoes and wipes the tissue along the edge of the black glass leaving a thin, white line cutting through the dirt. She nods, smiles and lifts her watch to her face and turns to me. I nod. It's time.

The following Wednesday, I stand poised behind the front door at 10:30 thrilled by my ingenuity. Having given it much thought over the week, I settled on the one saving grace available to me- my sense of humour. The door knocks, I tear it open and jump out at her from behind a plastic clown mask, watching and waiting for her face to crack open with unadulterated raw expression that I'm desperate to see.

The same neutral face looks back at me. I suddenly feel as if I've arrived at a fancy-dress party the only one in costume and fight the urge to say, "I'm not in" and close the door. Determined, I take out the joke book I had set aside by the door and leaf through the pages preparing to dazzle her with my comic wit. She reaches out and gently takes the book from me, placing it back on the side and shakes her head at me solemnly. I lift my hand to the mask that covers my face, suddenly afraid to lose the protection it offers me and she nods. I lift the mask off my face and place it in the bin by the front door feeling embarrassed. She nods and I watch her make her way up the stairs, feeling naked, wondering how on Earth I'll ever be able to keep her coming back.

We arrive at the foot of a familiar narrow corridor, the obscene graffiti glaring back at me from the wall opposite reminds me where we are. I blush at the obscenity that must be assaulting her eyes and wrap my arms around myself, feeling the dirty residue that still taints my skin from the last time I was here. I look at her with screaming eyes, struggling to control the tap-dancer taking up residency in my shoes. She looks at me, smiles and takes a step into the corridor looking back at me to follow. I shake my head at her and gesture to the open doors trying desperately to express the horrors that lurk beyond. In that moment I am catapulted to that last time walking down the corridor. I can feel those clutching hands and smell sour beer. My eyes are open but unseeing as I watch the film reel, grimacing with each finger tip that soils my skin. I desperately want to protect her from that evil, yet she smiles back unwittingly, not knowing what horror awaits her. Run! I shout in my mind, but the sound never makes it out of my lips. I watch, hand clamped over my mouth as she reaches out her hand, into the black, dark space through the doorway. Any minute now, the hands will come... they'll grab her. How will she fight them off? She is unprepared and unarmed...Half her arm now has disappeared into the dark abyss, then suddenly, she pulls... and she...... shuts the door.

She turns to face the next door and looks at me expectantly, smiling. I hesitate but lean out, pinch the handle and snap the door closed quickly, I laugh at the simplicity of it, the obviousness, feeling somewhat foolish, yet not really knowing why. We continue down the corridor until all the doors are closed. As each one closes, the corridor becomes lighter. At the end of the corridor she pauses to read the graffiti on the wall. A familiar blush tinges my cheeks and I look away as she reads the four words. She crosses to the corner of the room and rustles through the piles of junk on the floor. She returns with tins of paint and paintbrush and begins to cover the words with paint leaving the first letter of each word in place. I wait patiently behind her as she picks up the black paint and dabs at the wall, stepping back to admire her handiwork, she returns to my side, watching me as I read the capital letters before me:

PLACATE

TRAPPED

SELF-SABOTAGE

DANGER

Confused, I follow her back to the entry hall. She frowns as she notices the canvas sheeting that I have put back in place covering the far wall. I approach and reluctantly pull, exposing the empty frame once again. She hands me a tissue and nods at the frame. I shuffle awkwardly from one foot to the other and she nods again. She takes a step closer to me, scorching me with her proximity and gently takes my hand in hers. She places the tissue in my hand and together we slowly wipe the frame. Underneath the white line an unintelligible image is now visible. She looks at the frame and nods, lifting her watch and I see the hateful 11:50 blinking back at me. I follow her down the stairs and as she reaches for the door handle, I motion to her. I point at the dusty television on the side cabinet and raise my eyebrow at her questioningly, wishing immediately that I hadn't. She shakes her head solemnly, smiles, reaches for the door and I glare at the unruly pathway carrying her away not trusting that it will return her. I stand feeling naked, wishing I could take back the last five minutes and my last ounce of dignity that I just handed to her.

The next weeks pass by in much the same way and we find an unspoken rhythm. She continues to lead me in exploration of 'upstairs' and I file the questions that come up about her that always go unanswered.

One week she leads me into a vast, empty room; the only thing breaking up the sparse, bare walls are four doors opening off from each corner. I walk around the perimeter of the room and turn to see her watching me. I raise my shoulders and hands, palm upwards towards her when suddenly the doors slam shut around the room. The resounding echo reverberates, lifting me an inch from the floor. I run to the closest door, clasp the handle and pull at it frantically. It doesn't open. I run to the next door and turn the handle but that doesn't open either. I rattle the third and fourth doors in their frames with the same fruitless result. I steady myself against the dropping sensation in my stomach which leaves my organs in my throat. I rap my fists against the door and feel the rising puddle of acid sloshing inside me. My heart buzzes in my chest, the beats no longer discernible as the gaping chasm between my mind and reality widens. My body is no longer my own - an out of control car, Window-wipers, alarm, horn and lights blaring erratically and I don't have the keys. Noxious fluid oozes through my veins round my body which threatens to burst like an overinflated balloon. I am Dorothy in the cyclone and she is.........sitting cross-legged in the middle of the room, eyes closed, a picture of calm. 'How can she just sit there?!' I scream to myself. I want to shake the serenity out of her. I kick at each door and ram it with my shoulder, shouting out into the darkness beyond, but all I hear is my voice bouncing back to me. Still the girl sits silently in the centre of the room, offering nothing....'why won't she help me'? Her calm ignites a rage deep in my gut, how is she so unaffected? I scan the floor and ceiling tugging at my damp hair looking for somewhere to hide, terror tied to my ankle follows me round the room. I want to expel these feelings inside me out onto the floor, but I could not handle the shame. The moment has finally arrived, I'm about to fall apart, go over the ledge once and for all.......and she is going to see me do it!

I cower into the corner of the room, energy spent and knuckles raw. Tears fall down my face and I endeavour to squeeze myself into the nook of my arm as loud sobs ring out. My body shakes with the enormity of foreign feelings emanating through my pores, craving safe arms around me. I sob uncontrollably, keening wails echo across the room. I cry for as long as I ever remember doing so until I can take it no more. I have to make it stop! I lift my blotchy face and look across the room through bleary eyes. I stand up and approach the girl, still seated, eyes shut. "Ppp.. please help me" I stammer. Her eyes open and meet mine, there's a slight shift, a glimmer of something within them.... and then it's gone. She smiles exposing her white teeth that I don't remember seeing before and she nods at me and pats the floor next to her. I sit down, and she closes her eyes, I follow suit and am met with a powerful feeling that someone is going to punch me in the face. I open one eye to see if she is looking but she sits with her eyes closed, somewhere else. I close my eyes again and hear her rhythmic breathing injecting calm into the room around her. I attempt to mimic her slow, breathing but find this is a fundamental skill that has passed me by. It feels strained as if I have metaphorically lost the ability to tie my own shoelaces. My body fights me, tries to breathe in when I want to breathe out and I feel once again a failure as a human being... who can't breathe. Is she even still there?! Yes, I can hear her breathing.... Slow and steady. I shelve the inner critic and focus on the sound of her breathing and before long I am doing it! Oh no... I thought about it..... can't do it again. Again I focus on the sound of her breathing, steady and soothing. I feel the sensation in my nostrils as they welcome air, my lungs crinkling as they expand around the life-force. I can hear the thrumming of the pipes that snake under the floorboards beneath me. I breathe in to the knot that sits in my stomach pulsing with the beat of my heart. Everything quietens and slows. As time passes my eyelids gain weight and a pool of moisture builds at the corner of my mouth. A click interrupts the strains of my breath and my eyes transport me back into the room with a jolt. I wait for my senses to remind me where I am and stare open-mouthed at the doors standing open. The girl opens her eyes, smiles and stands, making her way to the doorway. She beckons me to follow and I stand reluctantly not wanting to shed the emotional duvet surrounding me. I follow down the corridor and, on our way out we pass the picture frame in the entryway. She takes out another gleaming white tissue and hands it to me. I place the tissue next to the white line of the frame and slide it meticulously across the solid glass, hoping it is neat enough. She nods and takes a step back admiring the picture with satisfaction. I take a step towards the picture and squint to make sense of the image in the smeary frame….. It looks like the edge of a face.

The girl lifts her watch to look at the time, raises it to show me and frowns as she realises I am no longer standing in front of her. I watch her scan the room puzzled until her eyes meet mine across the room. I stand in the doorway smiling, holding the door open for her to leave.

Weeks pass and we continue sorting through my mess. The girl sits patiently at my side as I work through the collection of 'stuff' I have amassed. At times I feel engulfed by the mammoth task ahead and question whether we are getting anywhere, but we push on, one step at a time, at my speed. We have become accustomed to one another now and have found our own ways of communicating wordlessly along a private mission that no one else would understand.

I know no more about her than I did when I first opened the door to the little girl with curly hair. I wonder about her often and she visits me in dreams where I beg her to tell me what her favourite song is…..but she never does. Without the stale, repetitive pleasantries and fake platitudes our relationship has become something different. There is a raw honesty and intensity, developed in a bubble beneath a microscope. Logically I don't know her at all, but on a different level I know everything I need to. Without any labels or boxes to put her in I have only the raw feelings flooding my veins and the way we interreact moment to moment to guide me. I navigate blindly with no handrails, but take comfort knowing I am moving forward. As the weeks go on I struggle to remember a time when she wasn't there. Some weeks her elusiveness frustrates me but I soon learn that I may *want* to know her favourite colour…. but I don't *need* to. Sometimes I want to keep her in my pocket and carry her around with me. Sometimes I feel we are playing a game that only one of us knows the rules to and I tread blindly terrified of breaking any. Each time she leaves I am filled with fear that this will be the last time. I have nothing to prove she will be there the following week, she owes me nothing and I can't fathom why she shows up each week... but she does. I have no idea what she thinks or feels about me and I often torture myself filling in the blanks. In absence of anything concrete, she becomes what I want her to be; a blank canvas for me to freestyle on each week. A strange paradigm... she is nothing to me and yet everything.

One week I follow her down the hallways as she strides ahead of me with purpose. We turn a corner and she stops waiting for me to catch up. I look at her questioningly. She moves aside and points to the far wall which houses a white door...... Number 26. I shake my head and turn to go, the siren within my body has begun to go off, rallying the troops. I feel the wave building within me, amassing energy and power with seemingly no outlet. I swallow to clear the large, dry brick in my throat. She looks across at the door and tilts her head to the side as if in question. I can't fathom where she gets this unfaltering belief in me and my abilities, but she overestimates me..... I cannot do this. I watch as she suspends bunched fists in front of her and slowly extends each finger from thumb to pinkie until she holds out ten splayed fingers in the air in front of her. She does this twice more, drops her hands, looks at me and nods and I realise the flames biting at my heels have receded ever so slightly. I nod back, take a deep breath and we walk slowly across the hall, the white grubby door looming before us. I take a big breath and look at her. She nods to me and I reach out my shaking hand and push the door. As my hand connects with the shabby wood there is a disturbance in the atmosphere. My senses alter as if I am listening through my eyes and watching through my ears. Like a television stuck between two channels yet trying to make sense of both. I take a step back, but my body remains standing in front of the door. I have become separated from my physical self. I look down at my feet then look at the body in front of me and realise it isn't my body at all. It's very much like mine, but a smaller version... a "Little-Me". I grip hold of my head in disbelief trying to decipher what is happening. I take another step back; 'Little-Me' remains by the door, hand pressed gingerly on the wood. I watch as 'Little-Me' timidly pushes the door and walks into the house. We follow on behind her, the pungent smell of urine and cigarette smoke chokes me and I cover my mouth to stop myself gagging. We watch from the doorway as 'Little-Me' enters the living room and sits down on the grubby sofa. Dirty nappies and toys litter the floor and wallpaper hangs half-stripped from the yellowed walls. 'Little-Me' sits hunched, hugging her knees, eyes darting from the blaring television to the window from which she can see her home just across the street. She is crying.

A cloud of smoke comes from a shirtless, bald, fat man sitting next to her on the sofa leering at her. The man sits in football shorts too small for him which ribbon into the fatness of his legs. His large gut hangs over the shorts onto the sofa and a sodden roll-up hangs out of his mouth feeding the smokey plume around him. He smiles at 'Little-Me'", exposing a mouth of blackened, yellowed teeth. His breath is stale and sickly. He pats the sofa next to him and pulls 'Little-Me' into him, she braces her body against him and lolls awkwardly into him. She shudders with the armpit hair that brushes against her shoulder and at the oniony tang that introduces her to body odour for the first time. Each part of her little body that is touching his feels tainted with a sticky, dirty film that she's not sure will ever come off.

I look down at 'Little-Me', her body frozen and mouth clamped shut. Her eyes telling a story of terror her voice can't find the words to. I know something bad is going to happen and though she doesn't know what it is, or what it will take from her...... so does she.

I turn to the girl standing beside me and point at 'Little-Me'. "You have to do something!" I say. She shakes her head solemnly, lifts her hand slowly and points at me. My eyes widen with recognition as I look back at her and she nods. I nod back. I stride into the room and kneel in front of 'Little-Me'. Her wide, watery, blue eyes meet mine and I feel like I might fall into them. I place my hand lightly upon her shoulder. She flinches at my touch but I keep a solid, constant pressure. What do you need Little one? I ask her. "Please take me away from here", she says as a a large tear slides down her blotchy face. She stands and her small, warm hand fits neatly into mine. We leave the detritus of that room behind us, walk through the door, neither of us looking back and pull it closed tightly behind us. I bend down and look into her eyes and put my arms around her tightly. I try to squeeze every ounce of love, care, warmth and safety that I can from my skin to hers and we stay there for some time… until she is ready to walk away.

The Three Musketeers walk side by side down the hallway- one whole and two halves. As we approach the entryway the girl stops outside a closed door, opens it and motions for me to follow. I really don't know if I can face any more doors today, but she is insistent. This room is strikingly different to the others I have been in. The room is softly lit by a floral lamp in one corner. A large woollen rug sits in the middle of the floor, brightly coloured, thick and welcoming. A framed picture of a Robin hangs upon the wall above an old gas fire cascading heat and a warm glow around the room. A little old lady sits in a corner of the room in a large, wooden chair which rocks backwards and forwards creaking in time with the carriage clock on the mantle. She has curly white hair, a round nose and deep brown eyes that twinkle behind glasses. She looks up and clutches her mouth in surprise as she sees us standing in the doorway and beckons us in. 'Little-Me' looks up at me and I nod to her. She runs across the room and jumps onto the old lady's lap, throwing her arms tightly around her neck in vice-like grip. The lady laughs and squeezes 'Little-Me' to her. She pulls a knitted quilt around her shoulders, enveloping 'Little-Me', a soft and squidgy human burrito as they rock backwards and forwards together. The lady strokes 'Little-Me's forehead in time with the rocking of the chair until 'Little-Me's eyes are heavy. I stand reluctantly and back towards the door quietly. The old lady smiles, blows a kiss across the room and I watch her brushing 'Little-Me's' hand with the edge of her thumb. I don't pull my eyes away from them both until the door closes in front of my eyes.

I bend down to catch my breath and find myself crying freely. Part of me wanted to stay in that room with them. The girl beckons me on and I follow back to the entryway where she leads me to the picture once again. She hands me a tissue and I repeat our now weekly ritual. A face is now partially visible in the picture frame though I can't tell if it is a boyish girl or a girlish boy. She reaches into her pocket and pulls out a stick of chalk. She bends forward and writes a word beneath the picture. She stands back looking pleased and watches me squint at the writing. My head jerks back to her frowning and I shake my head violently. I make a grotesque face mocking the face in the picture and a raucous giggle escapes from her mouth; a sacred exchange that feels like a million dollars. She shakes her head and points back to the word. I look at her frowning, bemused at the word written beneath the battered frame but she is a puzzle I have long since given up trying to solve.

Months pass. Every week she arrives on the dot at 10:30 and leaves at 11:50. I stop obsessing about her not showing up. A part of me just accepts that she will and that, in itself is the magic of her and me. I continue to sort through the carnage of upstairs as she looks on with interest and compassion. We return to the cupboard that once showered me in clutter all those months ago. This time I know what to expect and nimbly sidestep the junk that showers out above me. There is now one wall that contains boxes of items sorted and ordered.

Many boxes have been returned to their rightful owners. Some have been discarded and some have been taken downstairs and put on display. Though I still trip sometimes, it is easier to navigate now; the air is cleaner and easier to breathe. Each time she leaves, she stops by the frame on the wall, passes me a tissue and we expose another fraction of the picture in the frame. Each time she points at the word she has written underneath and, though I frown at her, I begin to warm to the girl in the picture who has become one of our triplet gang and feel guilty for having been unkind to her originally.

The following Wednesday I finish sweeping cobwebs, dust and broken glass into a neat pile in the corner of a room and pause leaning on the broom. The girl ushers me over to a wooden, circular table sitting in the centre of the room. A wooden box sits on the table. I look questioningly from the box to her. It is plain but has a circular hole in the top. She motions for me to put my hand inside the hole and I lay the broom down and place my hand into the box. I snatch my hand away as a sharp sting shoots up my finger. I shake my finger and inspect the tiny red dot forming on the tip. A tiny bubble of blood forms neatly as I squeeze it between my fingers. I point my finger towards her showing her my horrific injury, opening my hands out to her in question. She motions again for me to put my hand in the box. I look at her warily but shrug and push my hand back into the hole. I immediately pull my hand out and look incredulously at the other tiny speck of blood appearing at the end of my finger. I put it in my mouth and grimace as the tangy metallic taste lines the inside of my lips. I look to her for answers, but she gives me none. She indicates once again towards the box and I place my hand hesitantly back in and again tear it out, inspecting my now speckled finger. She watches me intently and then again indicates towards the box. I raise my eyebrows and look from her to the box and shake my head; 'what is she crazy?' Why does she continually want me to hurt myself?! Why would anyone do that?! I snatch at the edge of the table and push it aside. The table crashes over onto the floor, taking the box with it, which smashes into bits on the floor. She smiles.... Then nods at me which seems to constitute her approval then turns and leaves the room. I follow her out, scratching my head not entirely sure what just happened but feeling it was somehow important.

We make our way back to the entryway and stand looking at the picture frame together, our weekly homage. She points to the word once again beneath the picture. I tilt my head to one side and consider the now recognisable profile of a young girl. She's not exactly 'stereotypically pretty' but she has kind eyes and there is something nice about her. I smile and nod…. "Yes, I agree…. She is beautiful I say, "in her own way", I add quickly. She smiles back at me and clasps her hands together with the most expression I've seen from her yet. I watch, confused as she crosses the room to the large window where I once watched her arrive all those months ago.

She looks back at me and yanks at the thick, heavy curtain, currently blocking out the world. As the curtain falls to the floor, the room is enveloped in blinding bright light. I cover my eyes against the brightness, waiting for my vision to return. Sun pours in through the now bare window and I feel the warmth caress my skin as the light reflects onto the walls creating rainbow prism reflections.

The girl stands smiling at me and I suddenly feel I am missing something. I turn back to the picture frame upon the wall, now glowing with a metallic sparkle, glittering with refracted beams. It's beautiful. I walk closer to the frame, with the image of the girl and I notice that when my mouth drops open....... So does the girls.

It is then that I realise that it isn't a picture at all....... But a mirror.

The next week, I hurry down the stairs and pull open the door but stop short. The girl stands on the step in-front of me but this time she is not alone. She smirks at the surprise on my face as my eyes scan the familiar, smiling face of my partner. I look at the girl warily, not sure I want these two worlds to collide. She gifts me the same reassuring nod she has provided for what I realise now is 3 years. I cast my mind back to that first day and the mammoth task that stood before me. The years of rubbish to clear and damage to repair looked incomprehensible to me, but somehow her faith was unshakable. I smile and lead my partner by the hand up the stairs. I indicate the mat in front of the front door and she wipes her feet before following me in. I skip excitedly through the door and lead her round room by room. Pointing out the ornate etchings we uncovered on the oak bannister and photos that now adorn the walls. She smiles with encouragement and beams with wonder at the transformation of 'upstairs' and I see in her a pride that I can almost admit to feeling myself. 11:50 arrives and I raise my watch to show my partner. She understands and makes her way to the front door.

The following week the girl arrives and again is not alone. Standing behind her are a group of my closest friends. They smile at me holding up rollers and tins of paint and I usher them in. They wipe their feet and follow me upstairs as I share the work that I have been doing. I point out areas where loose floorboards still lay, and we find alternative ways to navigate around safely. They spend the day helping me cover the walls with brilliant White paint. After a few coats the cracks are barely visible, and we stand back admiring our workmanship. Everything looks crisp and fresh and I look round with gratitude at the warm faces around me. I lose track of the time and don't notice the girl letting herself out of the front door at 11:50.

The next week the girl arrives alone, and I lead her around upstairs and we both bask in the transformation. I lead her from room to room, pointing out the mirror that hangs in pride of place, the boxes sorted neatly against the wall. We laugh at the cupboard that once spat its contents at me and the repaired clock now hanging upon the wall, its ticking a reassuring comfort. As we turn each corner I can't help but wonder if we will come across number 26.... but we never do.

I lead her down a narrow corridor and point with pride at the new artwork hanging in the corridor. She smiles as she reads the blue painted words:

POSITIVITY

TENACITY

SELF-WORTH

DISCOVERY

As we make our way back to the entryway, as I so often do, I think of 'Little-Me' and the Old Lady's room. I know that they are gone from this place, but it doesn't stop me half looking for them. I know that they will remain safe together and that a piece of them will always be with me.

I lead the girl down the stairs and to the front door and she looks up at me, smiles and nods in the same way she always has. The instinct to embrace her never goes away as I watch her walk down the pathway and I settle instead for projecting every positive emotion I can onto her back instead… hoping that she might feel it.

I open the door the following week, my breath catching in my throat as I cast my eyes over the faces before me. Mum, Dad and my sister stand smiling back at me. Frowning, I return their smiles but step down and walk around them looking for something I already know is not there. As they look back at me, a little warily and bemused, my eyes acknowledge the glaring void far easier than my heart does. I glance up the well-trodden pathway that she passed down so many times, my mind reeling…..my breath catches in my throat as it dawns on me…..she is not coming.

My old friend panic makes an appearance, yet only serves to remind me how long it's been since I last felt that way.

I look up to the sky, in absence of knowing where she came from, or who sent her…"how will I do it without you?" I whisper…… "I never got to tell you….I"

"Thank you"….I whisper into the wind, swallowing the huge lump gathered in my throat.

I look back at my family gesturing to me and realise that there is more than one way to repay the little girl for all that she has given me. I take a big breath and place my hand over my heart, knowing she will remain there and nod, laughing to myself at the gesture.

I motion to my family to wait at the door and head back into the house. I rifle through the coats hanging on the hooks and put on my outdoor jacket. Grabbing my keys I swap my fluffy slippers for Red trainers and step out, closing the door behind me.

Closing my eyes, I lift my face up to the sun and fill my lungs with air. I watch my family walking down the path laughing with each other and run to catch up with them. I cast a look over my shoulder at the upstairs window where I stood all those years ago and think how grateful I am for the girl who kept coming back for me and for the strength I found to finally open the door.

Mon histoire n'a pas fini

Below is a poem I wrote to describe what it is to have cPTSD (for me).

It's…..

It's waking up each morning, feeling with all your soul that you won't be able to do that one thing today that you need to. The thing you've been doing every day for the last 2 years.

It's feeling embarrassed about the fact that you don't seem to function like the rest of the world.

It's reading Facebook post from friends and feeling torn- happy that they are on a plane, on their way to holiday or off to London for the night but hurting because you can't do those things.

It's dreading telling people you have holiday next week because they will ask- where are you going?

It's laughing at the text you get on a Friday night from a friend asking if you have plans. Wanting to respond with yes, I thought I'd take a train into London, get on a flight to Dubai, climb over the O2 arena but knowing you can't do any of those things and responding with the truth- I'm doing a jigsaw puzzle.

It's looking into the loving eyes of your wife seeing her desperation to understand and fix it, but knowing she can't and feeling guilty that you are giving her this burden.

It's opening your eyes in the morning, pulse racing, with a deep feeling of fear gripping you, despite praying the night before that tomorrow might be the day I wake up and it's gone.

It's telling yourself every five seconds of the day that it's irrational, illogical, no harm will come to you, you are safe, they are just thoughts but getting hoarse from repeating yourself when your body is deaf anyway.

It's dreading someone asking you to do something that will be out of your capability but dreading the day when they stop asking.

It's feeling like you are different from the world, like you are an imposter and terrified that one day your disguise will slip and they will see you for the fruit cake you are

It's trying to tell your Mum that not even she can make it better, in fact just her being there could even make it worse

It's feeling both under threat and a threat to the world. So out of control that you would be better away from everyone

It's wanting it to stop, being afraid to be alive but not wanting to die

It's being afraid of every moment that an obligation will arise that YOU CANNOT turn down, but you know you CANNOT cope with

It's feeling every episode that this time will be the time you lose your mind

It's eradicating your years of progress with one 'bad day' as your mind conveniently forgets all your successes but plays your struggles and difficulties on repeat.

It's wanting help but knowing you have all the help you can get and there's nothing else.

It's feeling about your thoughts the way you do about an annoying, unhelpful SATNAV.

It's knowing that ultimately, no-one can fix you.
It's being embarrassed that the lucky trusted few
have to be on standby in case you need them
knowing if they needed someone, they wouldn't call
you.
It's praying your Dad doesn't die because you can't
see how you will get to his funeral.
It's feeling engulfed by your shrinking world as
more and more things become off limits to you.
It's looking at the pictures of your nieces and
nephews on facebook wishing you could have been
there for that school play or that concert dreading the
time they find out Aunty Weewah is 'different'.
It's seeing traffic on the other side of the road and
worrying how you could get back home
It's scanning the side of the road for somewhere to
hide should the need arise
It's being petrified- not nervous butterflies but shit
yourself, kill yourself, make it stop petrified.
It's feeling like a failure as a wife, a friend, a sister, a
daughter and a patient.
It's feeling ashamed that someone else has to take
your wife to Thailand and pick her up at the airport.
It's worrying that one day going to work will
become 'out of bounds', people will become 'out of
bounds' and you will die in a puddle of your own
piss alone.
It's fundamentally feeling you don't have the
capacity to live your life.
It's praying you don't have some kind of accident
that warrants ambulance attention as you wouldn't
be able to get in the ambulance…. 'I'll just walk'
(With 2 broken legs)

It's feeling like there is no rescue.

It's smiling when people try to allay your fears of your car breaking down by saying 'you have AA right?! Knowing that you could never call AA if you needed to.

It's waking up every day and not knowing how you're going to get to work but getting up and doing it all the same. Never giving yourself the credit of your achievement because you're already thinking about having to do it tomorrow.

It's feeling everything is insurmountable

It's knowing that this is all 'in your head' and hating 'your head' for it

It's a voice louder than any rational or logical thought.

It's developing an absolute certainty that you CANNOT do something, even if you've done it before or there's nothing physically stopping you.

It's a mental wall

It's looking at photos of yourself thinking 'how the hell did I ever do that' and 'how the hell will I ever do that again'- Who is she?

It's feeling like a failure when your wheelchair-bound brother says 'you haven't been for a while'.

It's knowing you're wasting your life but feeling powerless to stop it.

It's doing everything 'right' and it still going 'wrong'

It's being afraid of people… especially yourself

It's worrying about something trivial such as a sick day and it manifesting into losing your job, your house, your wife, your life

It's mind over matter every second of your life

It's knowing that if you don't do it today... you might never do it again

It's having to psyche yourself out to go to a party but not 'I can't be arsed tonight' psyching but standing at the door of a plane with your parachute on everyone yelling at you to jump- trying to find that switch in your brain that can turn off the voice saying 'What the fuck are you doing?'

It's never knowing peace

It's never being on auto-pilot or subconscious

It's never losing sense of your mind for 5 seconds

It's feeling guilty, ashamed and a burden all the time

It's being ashamed to say all these things knowing that people are 'worse off' but wondering what could be worse...

It's thinking the worse possible thing that could happen in a moment and playing it on a loop in your mind- killing your wife, snapping the cats legs, dropping a baby, shitting your pants

It's knowing that it could happen ANYWHERE at anytime but still having the balls to step outside the front door and risking it anyway

It's being so convinced that you feel so out of control, you must therefore be out of control and therefore you will most certainly do something 'out of control' that you will never be able to take back

It's being afraid of people seeing you 'in the moment' and therefore cutting yourself off from any support or comfort when you need it most

It's wondering if they would be better off without you

It's jumping out of your skin when the door bell goes, convinced it must be the Police or someone to take you away

It's thinking in every conversation 'I would never cope if that happened to me' and building an ever growing list of insurmountable scenarios

It's wanting to live, to see, to dream, to explore to be free.

It's wanting to help, support and bring joy to other people and knowing you do the opposite

It's feeling useless, like a carcass.

It's the need for clarity, structure, organisation and calm.

It's constantly telling yourself tomorrow will be better and desperately looking for evidence that it is

It's feeling like everything is noisy and fast and intrusive.

It's wanting to find a space in the world where no-one is but knowing you couldn't get there anyway.

It's about finding ways to avoid feeling trapped and realising you can feel trapped in any situation if there's a helpful voice shouting- 'WE'RE TRAPPED, WE'RE TRAPPED- RUN FOR THE HILLS".

It's like running away from a firework tied to your leg.

It's wishing you were different

It's feeling guilty for being 'negative'

It's knowing your hope for recovery is therapy but in worrying so much that one day you won't get there, you don't get there.

It's putting so much pressure on yourself that you HAVE to do these things that you inevitably don't

It's worrying so much about letting someone down, that you do
It's wanting someone to tell you it will be ok and giving yourself the permission to believe them
It's feeling angry at your wife for 'arranging something'- another hurdle for you to jump but knowing she's not the one with the problem.
It's smiling when people say 'course you can you've done it before!'
It's feeling there's nowhere safe and nowhere to go
It's wanting to shout I KNOW! When people say if you don't do it… you'll only feel worse and wondering in that moment if there is a 'worse'.
It's an artificially created boundary that your mind created because when you needed to you didn't
It's a wall of safety that keeps people out but also keeps you in
It's also…

Having a crude perception that enables you to see people as they really are
Opportunity to appreciate your friends and family and the support they offer
Potential to educate and raise awareness
Enables you to be kind and compassionate to others by knowing struggle
Finding out you have people who really care
Unbelievable stamina and determination and refusal to give up
Learning more about yourself than anyone normally would and learning to accept it

It's frightening, It's hell on Earth but the end of my story will never be.... and so she gave up.

Acknowledgements

I am truly thankful every day for the wonderful people who have walked behind, beside or in-front of me on my journey. You have reminded me that there is good in this terrifying world. Mondy, my 'person'; knowing you always will be, without question is a gift I am incredibly thankful for. Ali- for being my 'Big Sis' when I let you. I hope one day you see your true reflection in the mirror. Mum & Dad- thank you for trying to learn to love my crazy. 'Aunty Helen'-For listening without judgement and keeping my words safe. Lauren- never underestimate the importance of your hugs or friendship to me. Jo- for your unfaltering support, for being willing to give me the clothes off your back and be my getaway driver. Michelle- For loving the dark and light in me, for embracing my journey and showing me 'everything's alright'. For making me believe that if I left you at the side of the road it would somehow be ok... I love you. Konstantina- for helping me to see a different ending to my story. I have achieved more than I thought possible because you saw it in me. You truly are a remarkable person. I am here thanks to you and glad about it because of you.

About the Author

Laura Hills-Garner lives with her wife and two Dogs (Cats) in Essex. Laura is a Supply Chain Professional and uses writing as a mechanism to cope with cPTSD (Complex Post Traumatic Stress Disorder) and GAD (Generalised Anxiety Disorder). She is a published poet and author of the blog: 'imtheonein4.wordpress.com'. 'Upstairs' is her first published story.

10% of all proceeds donated to 'Mind' charity

Printed in Great Britain
by Amazon